Living by Faith:
An Adult Coloring Book of
Inspirational Poetry

Copyright ©2018
Jeaninne Stokes
JStokes Publishing Company
Scripture quotations
are taken from the
Holy Bible New Living
Translation ©1996, 2004, 2015
by
Tyndale House Foundation
Used by permission of
Tyndale House Publishers, Inc.
Carol Stream, Illinois 60188.
All rights reserved.

Artwork and cover design by
Deborah Muller

Today's Faith

The faith today that lives in me
Is no longer the faith that used to be
For as I've walked with
the Master each day
And as I've learned to
yield and pray
With each new day
and passing year
Old faith is gone;
a new faith is here
My life is no longer
as it was before
Like an eagle on high,
my faith has soared.

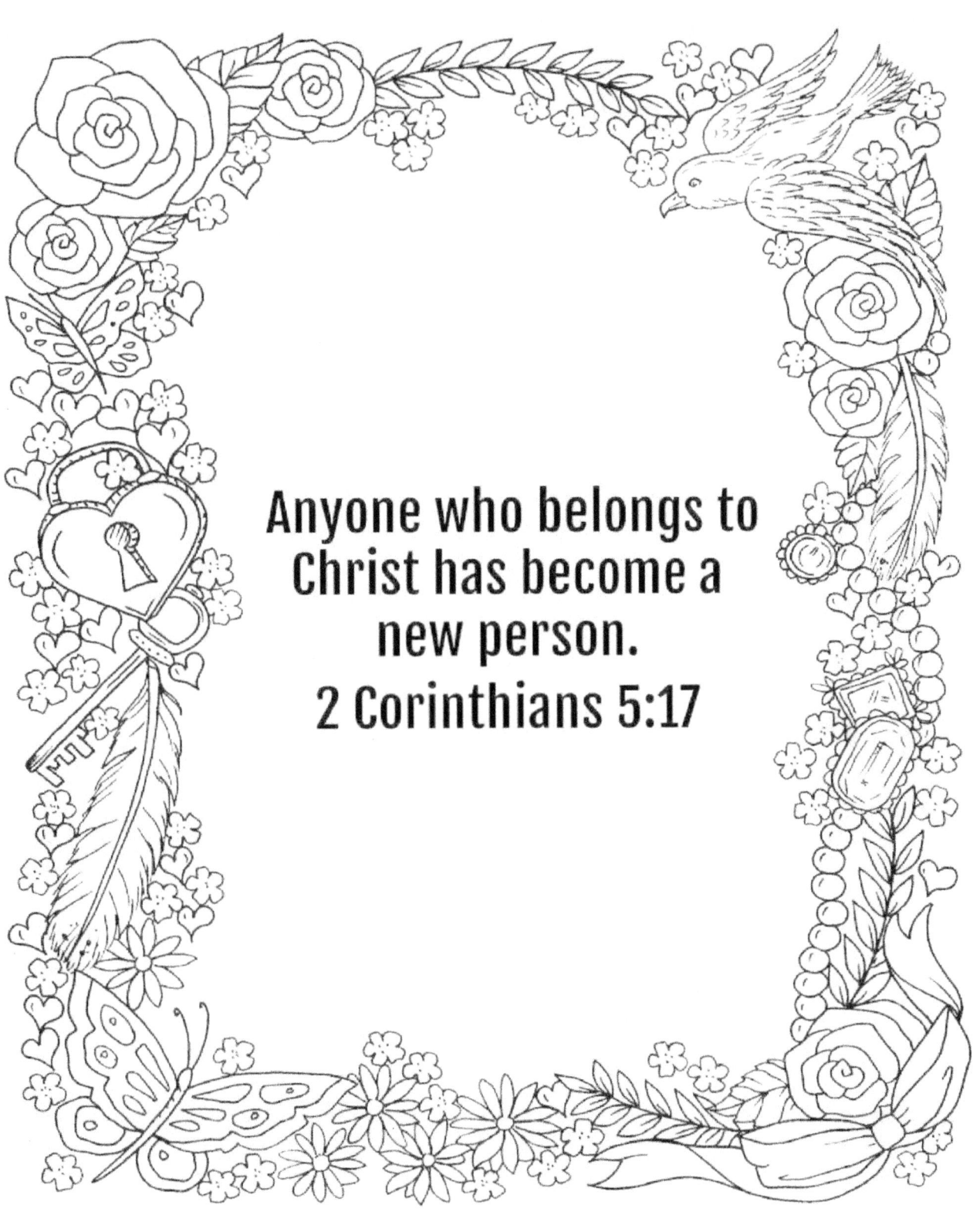

Come Home

It doesn't matter how far you stray
For God still hears you when you pray
And He will wash away your sins
If you will just come home to Him.
So if you've wandered far away
And wondering what to do today
Confess to God the life you've missed
And come on home to restfulness.

WHEN GOD SEEMS SILENT

Your Father is concerned about all your cares
And hears your deep and earnest prayers
And His silence is never as it seems
For He's still working behind the scene
Just trust His timing and trust His Word
And believe all of your prayers are heard
For no matter how long it seems to take
His answer is never, ever late.

The Sabbath

There is a day that's in the week
We should honor and always keep
A day to worship and to rest
And to renew our souls afresh
A day to honor the one above
And give him thanks for all he does
So guard this day with all your heart
And keep it holy and set apart
And wonderful blessings the Father will give
To those who keep this one day His.

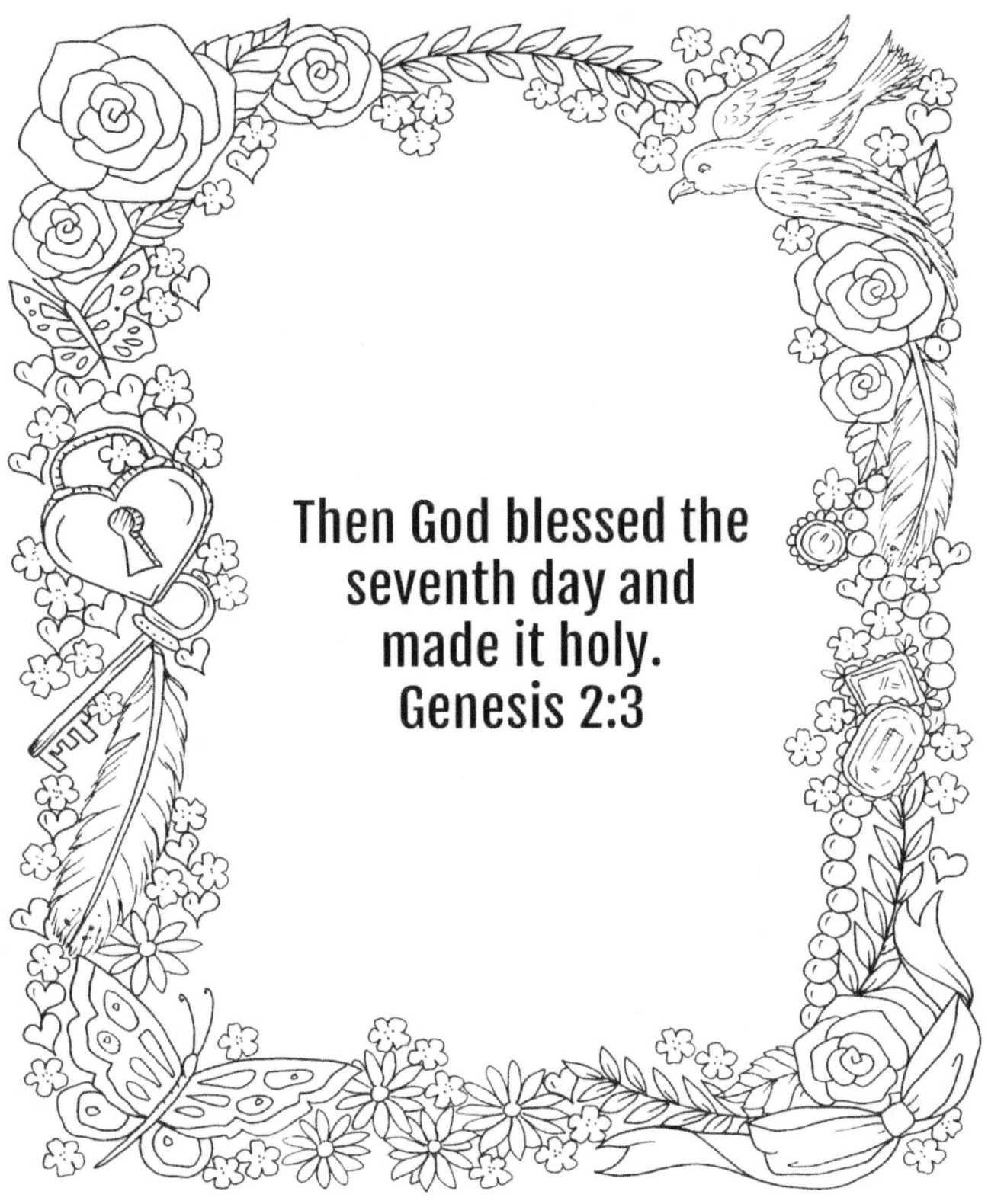

Don't Worry

You told me not to worry about the cares of life today
For you will take good care of me like you did yesterday
You told me not to worry when life seems to go awry
For every need I have today you've promised to supply
So I've decided not to worry over what the day may bring
What I will eat or drink or wear along with other things
As you take care of every bird that glides
throughout the air
I know you'll take good care of me,
no matter what the care.

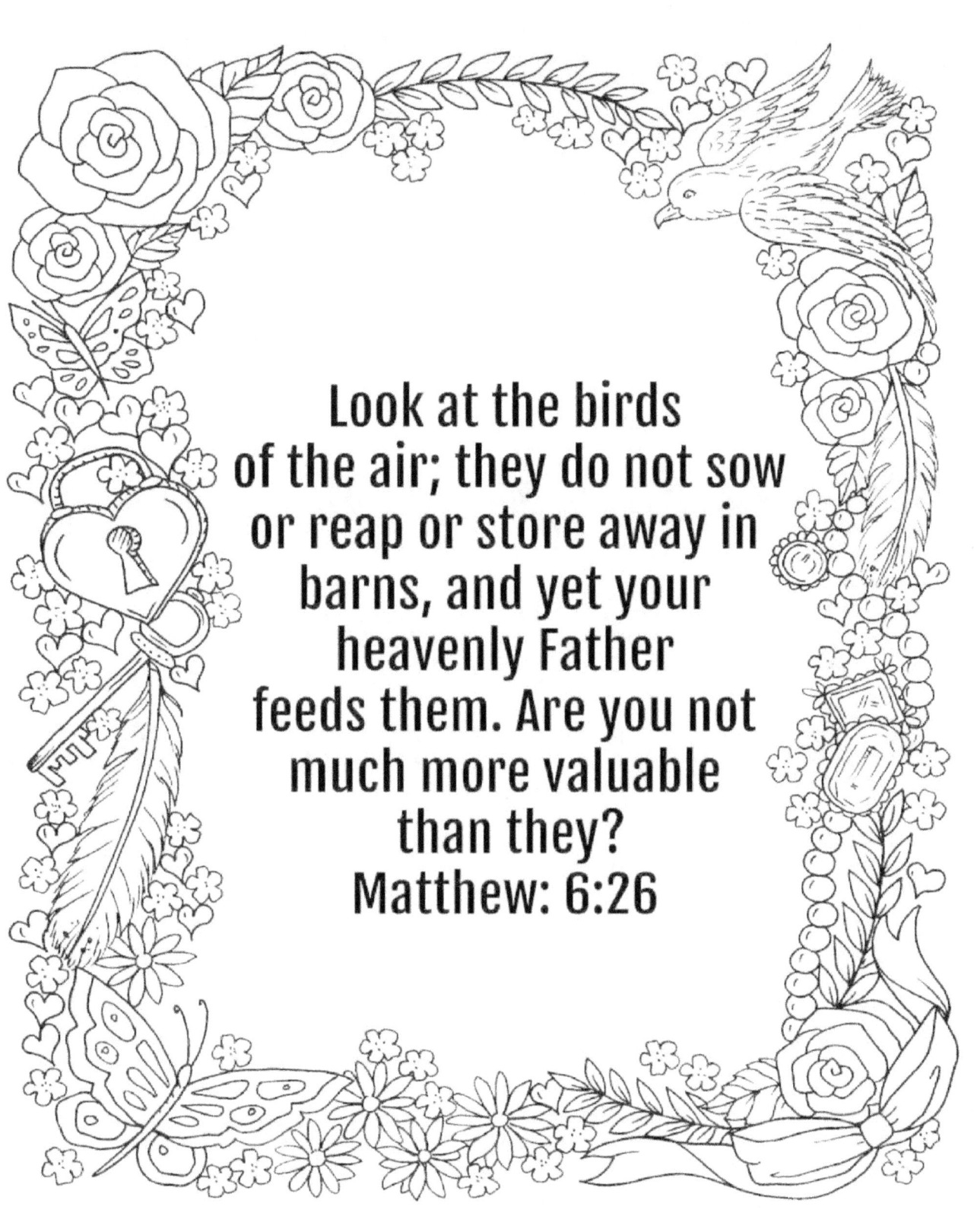

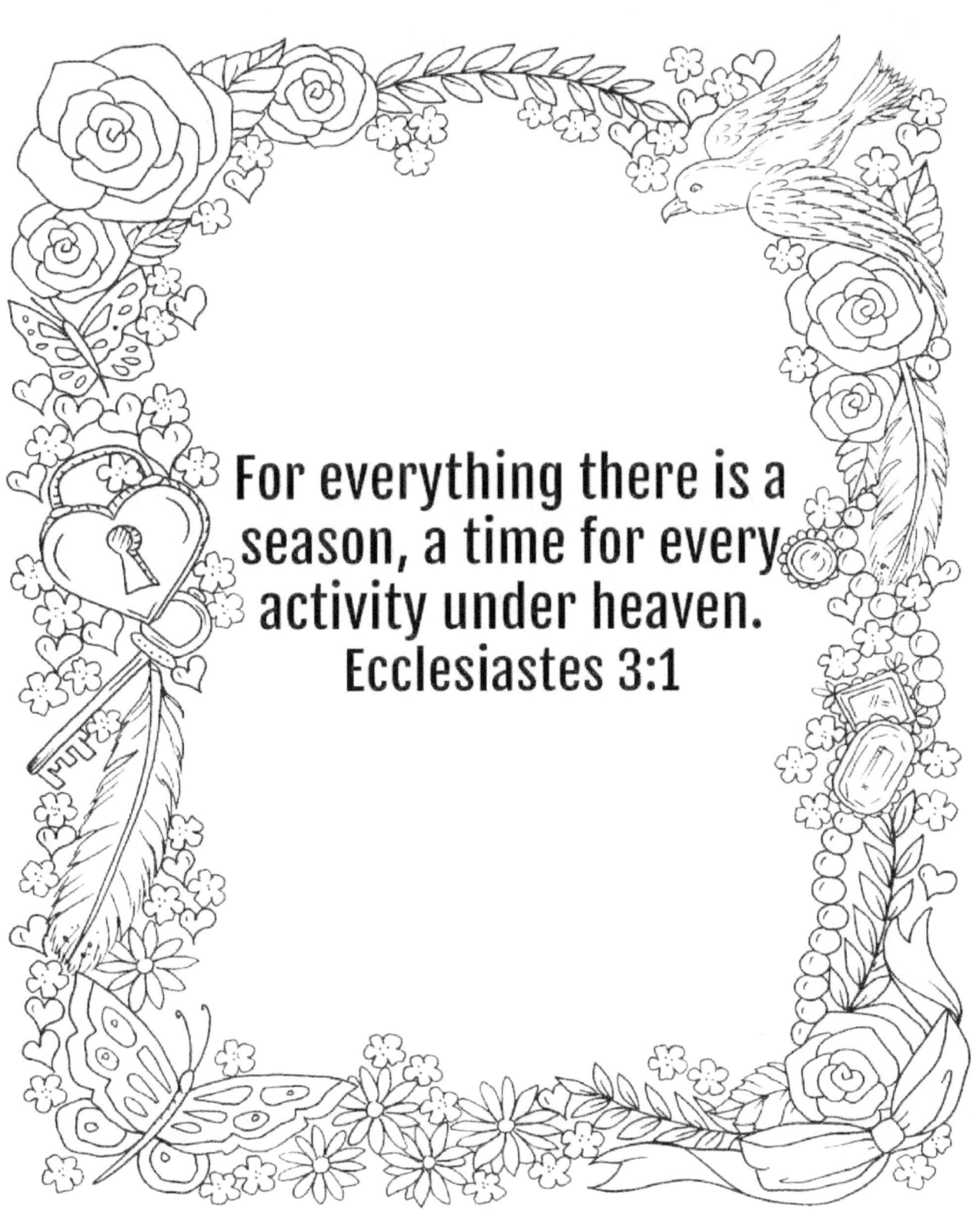

Where?

You may look to the hills to find your help there
To ease all your worries and ease all your cares
You may look to the skies covered freshly in blue
To find there an answer for all you go thru
But there's only one place that you should look to
And it isn't the mountains or the skies painted blue
Just look far beyond when you're tattered and torn
And you'll find that your help will come straight from the Lord.

The Treasure

When I open the Word to read every day
I find hidden treasures along the way
For nestled between every page and line
Are jewels of joy and peace of mind.
I'll cherish the Word from beginning to end
For it teaches me how to live and to stand.
And I'll hide it deep in the recess of my heart
For that's the one place it will never depart.

The Battle

There's a battle going on
in the world you live in
It's a powerful battle
against the army of sin.
There are heavenly forces
that are on the attack
But with God's holy armour,
you can fight them all back
Use the sword of the spirit
for every battle you fight
To ward off the demons
with all of your might
And no matter how long you face
the battle with sin
If you're wearing the armor,
you are destined to win.

We are fighting against evil rulers and authorities of the unseen world. Ephesians 6:12

Here I am again

I'm glad it never matters
How many times I pray
For the Father always listens
And will never turn away.
So here I am again
And glad to know I'll find
Each time I give my cares to God
He gives me peace of mind.

Stillness

When life overwhelms us and we've had our fill
Those are the times we are called to be still
To take just one moment - one slither of time
So we can hear clearly from the heavens divine
If we are willing to listen and willing to yield
And willing to answer the call to be still
We'll receive inner power to face a new day
And the courage to face what
may come our way.

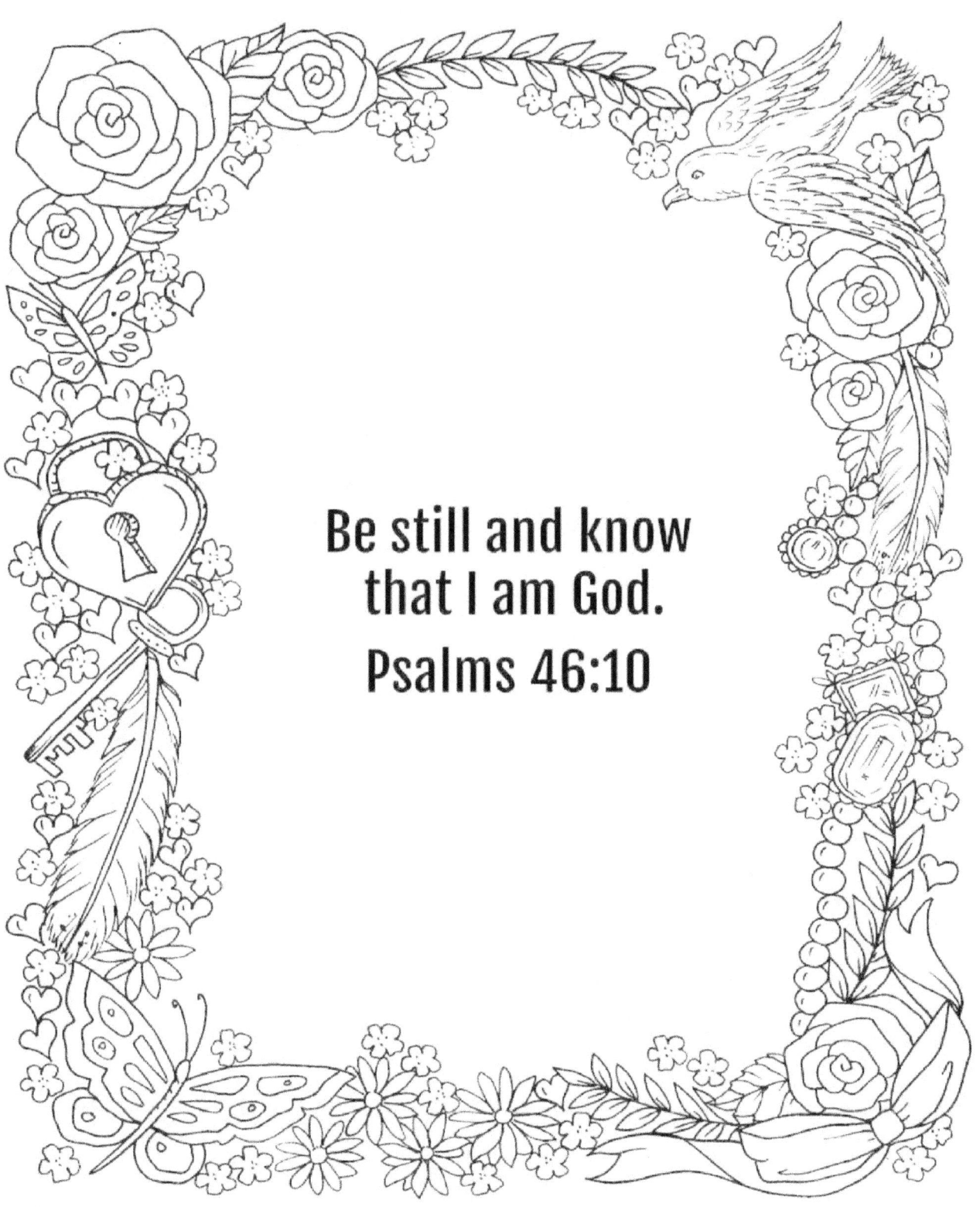

Be still and know that I am God.

Psalms 46:10

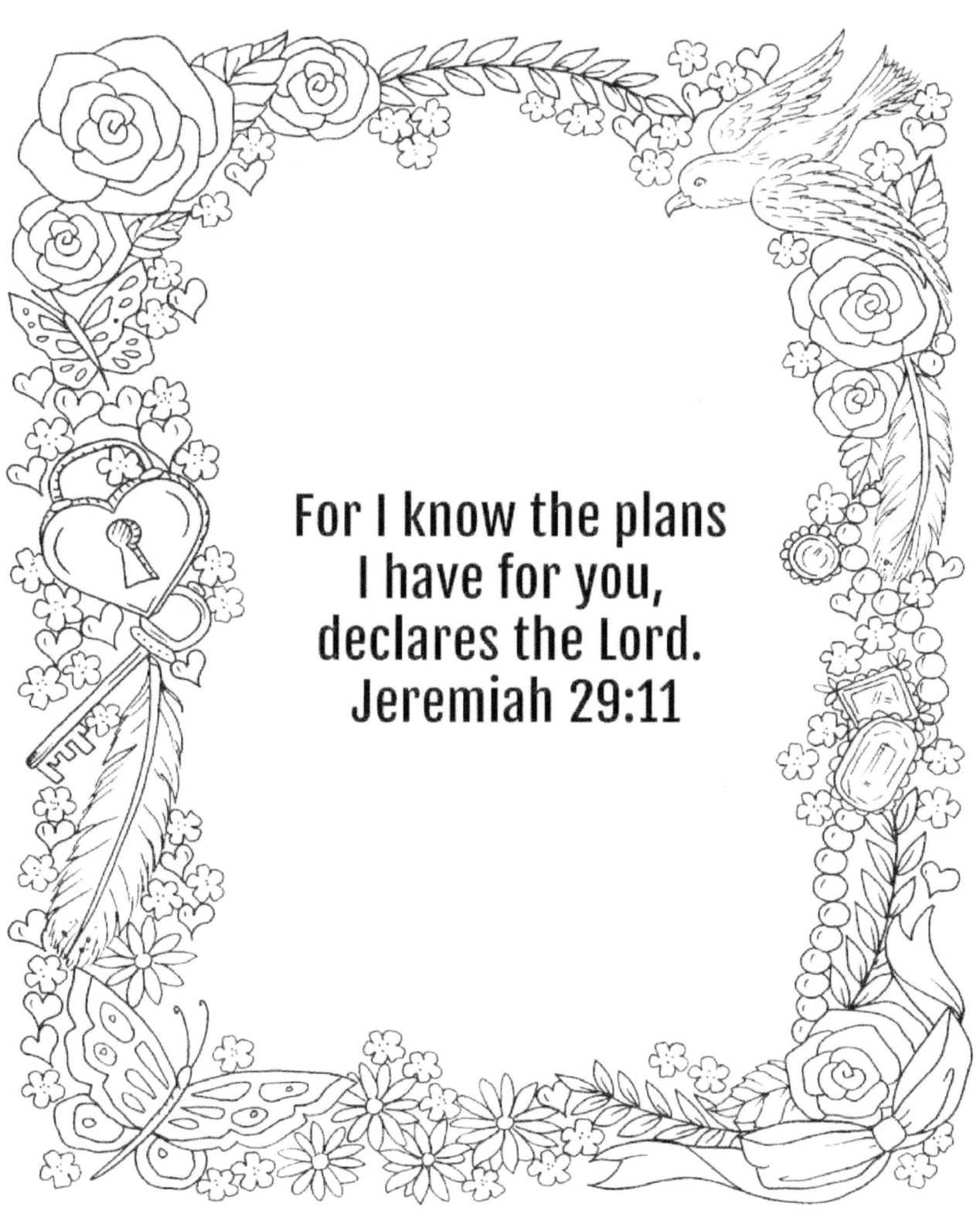

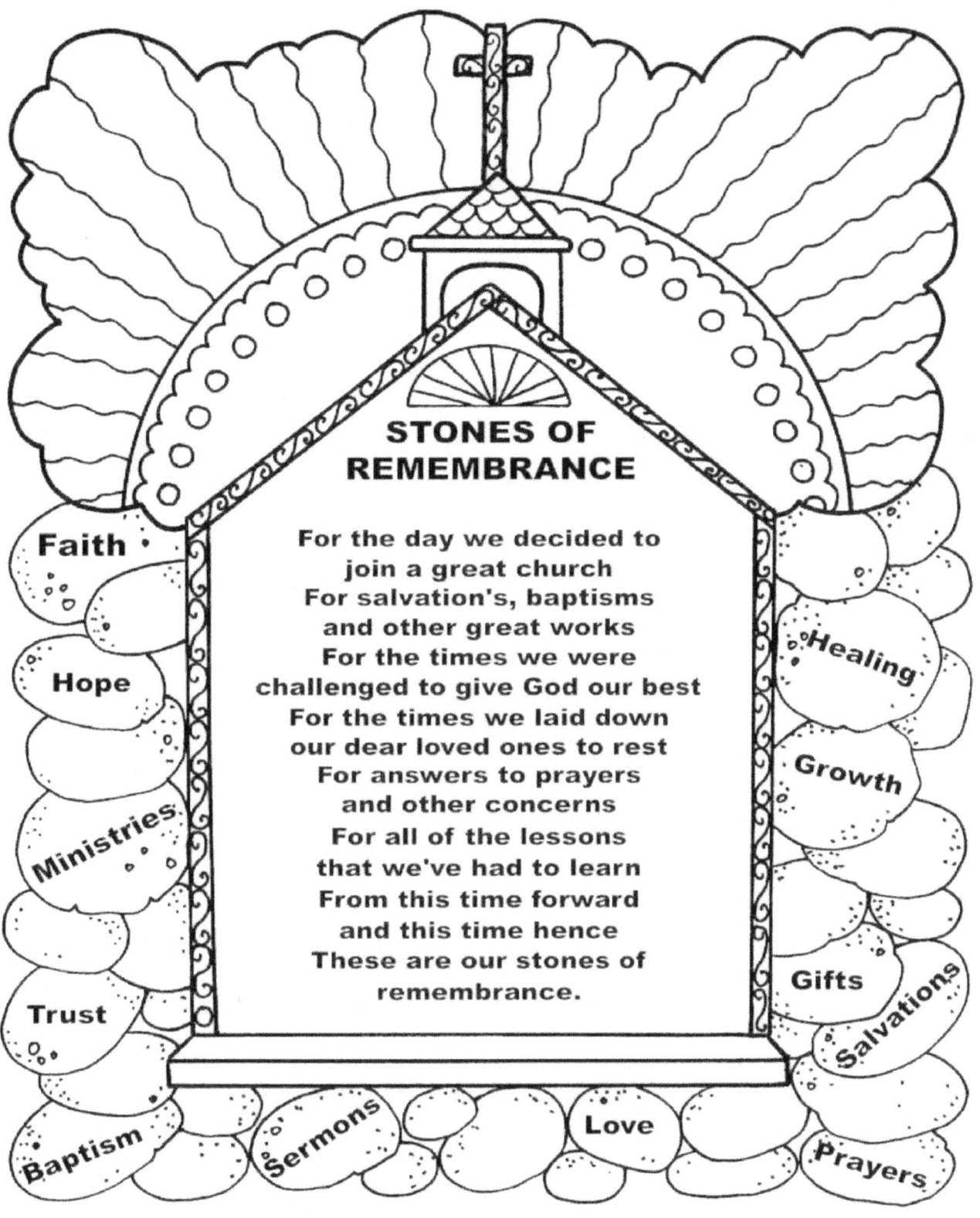

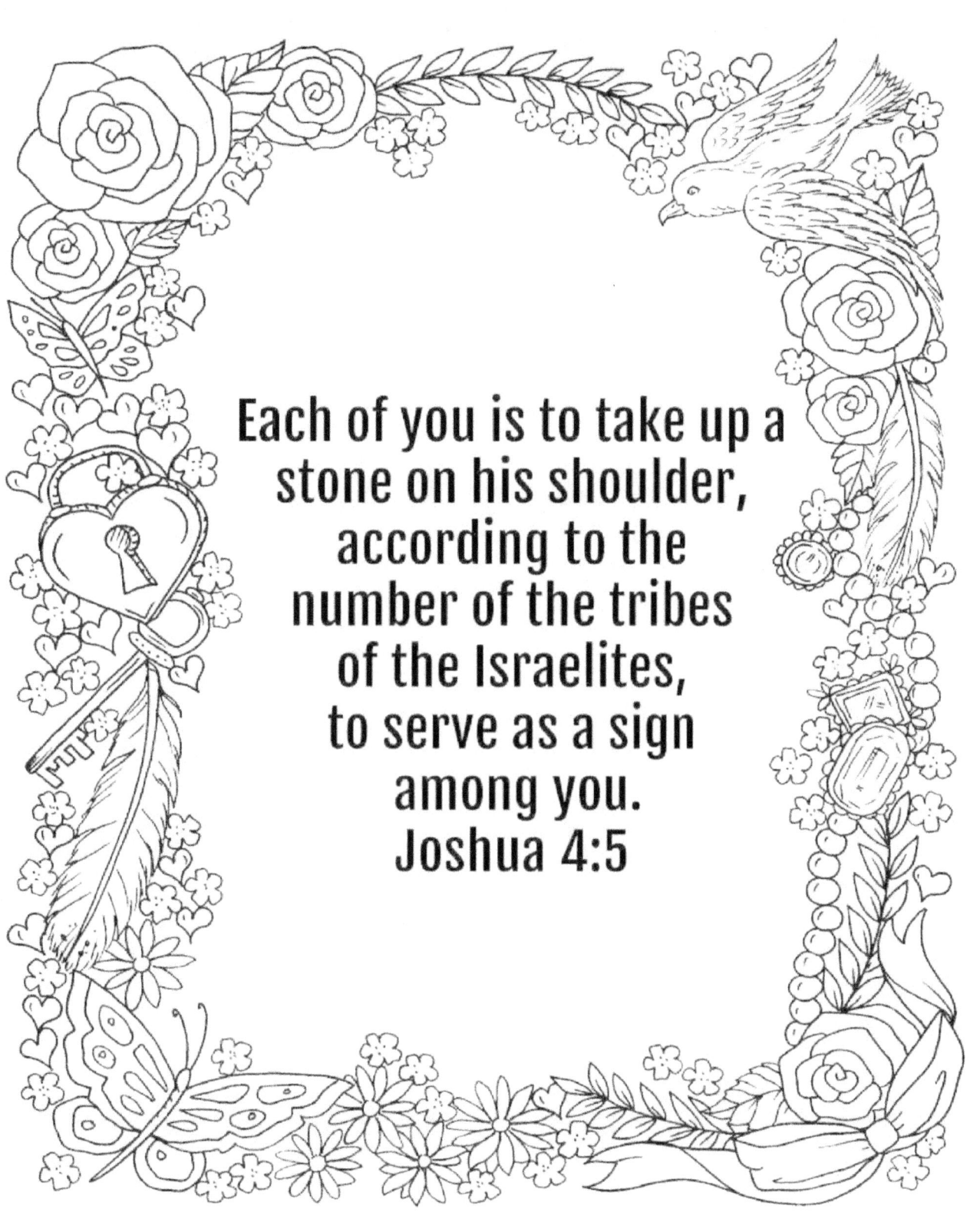

Each of you is to take up a stone on his shoulder, according to the number of the tribes of the Israelites, to serve as a sign among you.
Joshua 4:5

Grace to Grace

When life gets dark, just like the night
And we are ready to give up the fight.
It's by His grace we'll tunnel on
Until the day He calls us home.
For grace to grace is what He gives
It's in his power that we live
Each time we think we can't go on
That's when by grace,
He makes us strong.

My grace is sufficient for you, for my power is made perfect in weakness.
II Corinthians 12:9

www.ingramcontent.com/pod-product-compliance
Lightning Source LLC
Chambersburg PA
CBHW081156290426
44108CB00018B/2577